SUPER COOL
SCIENCE AND ENGINEERING
ACTIVITIES
WITH MAX AXIOM Super Scientist

by Agnieszka Biskup
and Tammy Enz

Table of Contents

Chapter 3 66

Chapter 4 96

Inside his high-tech laboratory, Super Scientist Max Axiom receives an important video message.

BEEP!

PLAY

Hello, Max. Mayor Richardson here.

As you know, the city's very first science and engineering conference opens this weekend.

A major part of that conference will be a student activity lab.

This lab must allow students to test their science and engineering skills with hands-on activities.

But the conference staff is running out of time.

And they haven't gathered the variety of activities we need.

I need your help, Max Axiom. The conference is counting on you.

4

Sounds like a big problem.

Luckily, my lab's secret files are loaded with activities related to chemical reactions, forces and motion, and mechanical and structural engineering.

- 37 science and engineering activities
- Common household materials
- Utility knife, drill, and other basic tools
- Gloves, goggles, and other safety gear
- Lab notes sheets

With a little planning, I'll give the science and engineering conference exactly what it needs.

Now that I know what I need to gather, I can't wait to get to work. These activities are going to be a blast!

Come on. Our first stop is a campfire to kick off chemical reactions.

WITH MAX AXIOM

BUBBLING BLOBS

Oil and water don't mix, and this project uses that fact to its advantage. Check out how a chemical reaction can create a super cool lava lamp.

YOU'LL NEED

clear, clean plastic 16.9-oz. (500-mL) drink bottle

vegetable oil

water

food coloring

effervescent tablets

PLAN OF ACTION

1. Fill the bottle three-fourths full of vegetable oil. Then slowly pour water into the bottle until it's almost full.

2. Wait a few minutes for the oil and water to separate completely.

3. Add about 12 drops of food coloring.

4. Wait for the food coloring to fall through the oil and mix with the water on the bottom.

5. Break an effervescent tablet into three or four pieces, and drop them into the bottle.

6. Watch the blobs begin to rise!

⚡ AXIOM EXPLANATION

The effervescent tablet reacts with the colored water to form bubbles of carbon dioxide gas. The gas rises and takes some of the colored water with it. The gas escapes when it reaches the top of the bottle. The colored water droplets then fall back down into the bottle.

ENDOTHERMIC BAGGIES

Some chemical reactions absorb energy and decrease the temperature of their surrounding environment. Try this experiment to feel the effects of an endothermic reaction as it happens in the palm of your hand.

YOU'LL NEED

1 teaspoon (5 mL) citric acid*

1 teaspoon (5 mL) baking soda

1-quart (1-liter) zipper-type plastic storage bag

water

*found at health food stores or at supermarkets with canning supplies

1. Pour the citric acid and baking soda into the plastic bag.

Baking Soda

Citric Acid

2. Shake the bag gently to mix the two ingredients.

3. Pour a small amount of water into the bag and seal it quickly.

4. Hold the bag in the palm of your hand as the chemical reaction takes place.

AXIOM EXPLANATION

Citric acid, baking soda, and water react to produce carbon dioxide. The gas fills and inflates the bag. Because the reaction is endothermic, the liquid in the bag becomes cold to the touch. Once the reaction ends, the mixture returns to room temperature.

MONSTER TOOTHPASTE

When it comes to chemical reactions, the most exciting ones are often exothermic reactions. They can produce energy as heat—sometimes in surprising ways. Monster toothpaste is one exothermic reaction that never fails to wow a crowd.

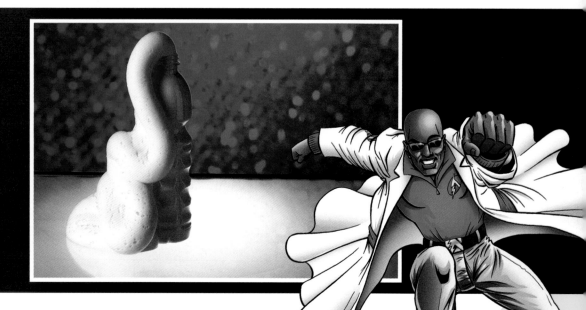

YOU'LL NEED

small bowl

packet of dry yeast

3 tablespoons (45 mL) of warm water

clear plastic drink bottle

foil roasting pan

½ cup (118 mL) of 6% hydrogen peroxide*

liquid dish soap

food coloring

funnel

*found in beauty supply stores or hair salons

SAFETY FIRST

Put on gloves and safety goggles before trying this experiment. Hydrogen peroxide can irritate eyes and exposed skin.

PLAN OF ACTION

I. Mix the yeast and warm water in a small bowl.

2. Set the mixture aside for about 30 seconds, or until the liquid becomes frothy.

3. Place the plastic bottle upright in the center of the roasting pan. Ask an adult to pour the hydrogen peroxide into the bottle.

4. Put two or three squirts of liquid dish soap into the bottle.

5. Add about 5 drops of food coloring to the bottle.

6. Gently swirl the bottle to mix the ingredients and return it to the center of the pan.

7. Using the funnel, pour the yeast solution from step I into the bottle.

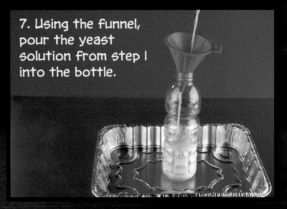

8. Quickly remove the funnel, stand back, and watch the monster toothpaste ooze out!

⚡ AXIOM EXPLANATION

The yeast speeds up the chemical reaction that breaks hydrogen peroxide into oxygen gas and water. The dish soap traps the oxygen, resulting in the formation of foam bubbles. The foam is basically soap and water, so it's safe to touch. Because this is an exothermic reaction, the bottle and foam should feel warm.

MINI MAGIC FIRE EXTINGUISHER

A fire will keep burning as long as it has fuel, oxygen, and heat. This chemical reaction removes one of those ingredients to put out a fire.

YOU'LL NEED

3 votive candles

matches

2-quart (2-liter) clear glass pitcher

2 tablespoons (30 mL) of baking soda

I cup (225 mL) vinegar

SAFETY FIRST

Be sure to ask an adult for help using candles and matches before doing this activity.

PLAN OF ACTION

1. Place the candles in a row on a flat surface in an open area outside. Ask an adult to use the matches to light the candles.

2. Place the baking soda into the pitcher.

3. Pour in the vinegar. Swirl the pitcher so that the ingredients are well mixed. The mixture will fizz and foam.

4. Slowly tip the pitcher near the candles without spilling any liquid. Watch what happens to the candle flames.

⚡ AXIOM EXPLANATION

When vinegar and baking soda mix, the chemical reaction forms carbon dioxide gas. Carbon dioxide is heavier than air, so it will stay in the pitcher longer while it's upright. When the pitcher is tipped over the flames, the carbon dioxide pours out. It sinks down over the candles, pushing the oxygen out of the way. The flames go out because a fire can't burn without oxygen.

EGG-CELLENT EGGSPERIMENT

What does an egg look like without a shell? Find out with a chemical reaction with the power to make an eggshell disappear.

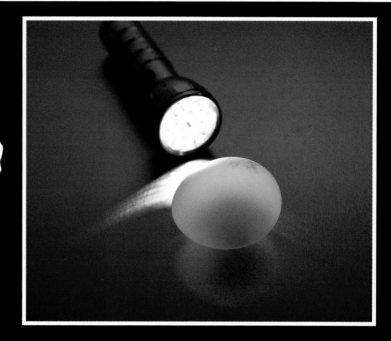

YOU'LL NEED

1 raw egg

clear glass jar with lid

vinegar

flashlight

1. Gently place the egg in the jar.

3. Let the egg sit in the vinegar for 24 hours at room temperature.

4. Use the lid of the jar to gently strain the vinegar into a sink. Be careful to not let the egg fall out of the jar.

2. Add enough vinegar to completely cover the egg. Screw the lid on the jar.

5. Cover the egg with fresh vinegar, and let it sit undisturbed for another two days.

7. Shine a flashlight through the rubbery egg to see the yolk.

6. Carefully remove the egg from the vinegar. Gently rinse it with water.

⚡ AXIOM EXPLANATION

You may have noticed tiny bubbles all over the egg in the vinegar. These bubbles were carbon dioxide gas. They were produced by a chemical reaction between the vinegar and the egg shell. Vinegar, which contains acetic acid, reacted with the eggshell to dissolve it.

FUNNY BONES

Bones are hard and typically break if you try to bend them. This chemical reaction will give you bones that behave in funny ways.

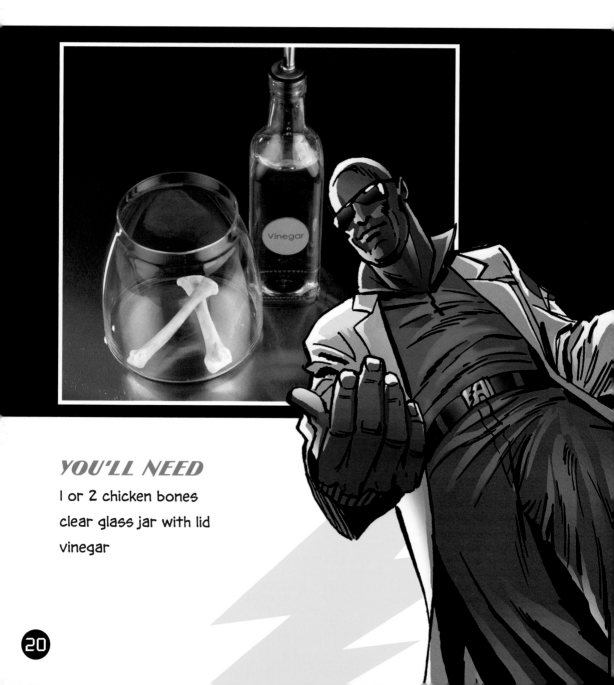

YOU'LL NEED

1 or 2 chicken bones

clear glass jar with lid

vinegar

PLAN OF ACTION

1. Rinse and clean the bones with warm water to make sure all the meat has been removed.

2. Let the bones dry. Note that the bones are hard and do not bend.

3. Place the bones in a jar.

4. Add vinegar to the jar to completely cover the bones. Place the lid on the jar.

5. Let the bones sit for at least 3 days.

6. Remove the bones from the vinegar.

7. Try to bend the bones now. Do they feel any different?

⚡ AXIOM EXPLANATION

Bones contain calcium and phosphorus. These minerals make bones strong and hard. The acetic acid in the vinegar reacts with the minerals. It leaves the remaining materials in the bone soft and rubbery.

POLISHED PENNIES AND COPPER NAILS

Have you ever noticed that pennies turn darker with age? It's all because of chemical reactions. In this two-part experiment, you'll make some old pennies look new again while turning others a little green! You'll also make a steel nail look like copper.

YOU'LL NEED

glass or plastic bowl
(not metal)

¼ cup (60 mL)
of vinegar

I teaspoon (5 mL)
of salt

plastic spoon

20 old, dirty
copper pennies*

paper towels

marker

kitchen timer

2 clean steel nails

*For best results, use
pennies minted before
1982—they contain
more copper than
pennies today.

1. Pour the vinegar into the bowl.

2. Add the salt to the vinegar, and stir it with a plastic spoon until the salt dissolves.

3. Put all the pennies in the bowl.

4. Wait about 5 minutes, then take all the pennies out of the bowl. They should look shiny. Set the bowl of vinegar aside for part two of this experiment.

5. Place 10 of the pennies on a paper towel to dry.

6. Rinse the other 10 pennies under running water, and place them on another paper towel to dry. Write "rinsed" on that paper towel with a marker so you know which is which.

Rinsed

7. Set the kitchen timer for 1 hour and leave your rinsed pennies to dry. In the meantime, proceed to part two of this experiment.

PLAN OF ACTION PART TWO

1. Submerge one steel nail into the leftover salt/vinegar liquid.

2. Place the other steel nail half-in and half-out of the liquid by leaning it against the side of the bowl.

3. Let the nails sit for the remainder of the time left on the kitchen timer you set in part one.

4. When the timer goes off, check to see how your pennies and nails look.

⚡ AXIOM EXPLANATION

New pennies turn a dirty brown over time because copper reacts with oxygen in the air. A dark substance called copper oxide forms on the surface. The acetic acid in the vinegar removes the copper oxide from the pennies, making them bright and shiny again.

Rinsing the pennies under water stops the chemical reaction. The salt/vinegar mix left on the unrinsed pennies allows the chemical reaction to continue, forming a blue-green chemical coating.

The vinegar/salt solution removed some of the copper from the pennies, which remains in the liquid. When the steel nails are placed in the liquid, the copper is attracted to the metal of the nail. You end up with copper-coated nails!

LACTIC PLASTIC

In the early 1900s, casein plastic was used for jewelry, buttons, combs, and buckles. Surprisingly, this plastic was made with ordinary cow's milk. With a simple chemical reaction, you can make your very own casein plastic.

YOU'LL NEED

I cup (225 mL)
of whole milk

small pot

small bowl

4 teaspoons (20 mL)
of vinegar

food coloring

spoon

fine mesh strainer

large bowl

paper towels

continued

n adult to heat the milk in a
the stove. Heat until the milk
hot but not boiling.

an adult pour the hot milk
mall bowl.

3. Add the vinegar and 5 drops of
food coloring to the milk.

4. Stir the mixture slowly with
a spoon for about a minute.

5. Carefully pour the milk
through the strainer into
a larger bowl. A bunch of
clumps should remain in the
strainer. Pour any liquid in
the bowl down the drain.

Let the clumps cool for a few minutes. Place them on a paper towel, and press them gently with another paper towel to soak up any extra moisture.

7. Knead the clumps together with your fingers to make a ball. You have just made a ball of casein plastic.

8. Mold your plastic into any shape you want.

9. Set your molded plastic on a plate to dry and harden for two days.

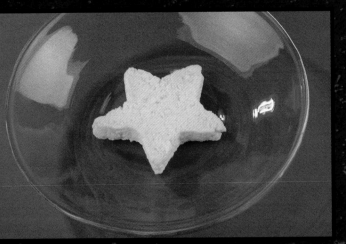

AXIOM EXPLANATION

Milk is full of a protein called casein. The combination of heat and acetic acid from the vinegar makes the milk curdle. This process pulls the casein proteins out of the milk to form rubbery clumps called curds. The casein curds make up the plastic you can form into various shapes.

GLUE GOO

Sometimes chemistry can get a little gooey. Create a homemade version of slime by using the power of cross-linking molecules!

YOU'LL NEED

2 plastic disposable cups

1 teaspoon (5 mL) of Borax powder*

½ cup (118 mL) of water

plastic spoon

½ cup (118 mL) of white craft glue

food coloring

glass bowl

*found at the supermarket near the laundry detergent

PLAN OF ACTION

1. Add the Borax powder and half of the water to a plastic cup. Stir well with the plastic spoon, then set aside.

2. Pour the glue into a second plastic cup.

3. Add the remaining water and a few drops of food coloring to the glue.

4. Use the plastic spoon to stir the glue-water mixture well.

5. Pour the contents of both cups into the bowl. Stir well. The slime will form before your very eyes.

6. Let it sit for about 30 seconds before you pull it out to play with it. Put the slime in a sealed plastic bag to keep it from drying out.

AXIOM EXPLANATION

White craft glue is a polymer. It is made up of long chains of molecules of a substance called polyvinyl acetate. The chains easily slip and slide against each other, allowing the glue to be poured. When you add the Borax and water solution to the glue, a chemical reaction occurs. The long glue molecule chains get cross-linked together to form the rubbery, stretchy, gooey stuff we call slime.

MAGIC COLOR CHANGE

Sometimes a chemical reaction can look like magic. This show-stopping experiment has an astounding color change that happens in the blink of an eye!

YOU'LL NEED

2 500-milligram vitamin C tablets*

plastic sandwich baggie

metal spoon

measuring spoons

3 disposable clear plastic cups, labeled "1," "2," and "3"

warm water

plastic spoons for stirring

1 teaspoon (5 mL) of 2% tincture of iodine*

1 tablespoon (15 mL) of 3% hydrogen peroxide*

½ teaspoon (2 mL) of liquid laundry starch

stopwatch

*find these items at a pharmacy or drugstore

SAFETY FIRST

Remember to wear safety goggles and gloves while handling iodine and hydrogen peroxide in this experiment.

1. Place the vitamin C tablets in a plastic baggie. Crush them into a fine powder using the back of a metal spoon.

2. Pour the crushed powder into Cup 1. Then add 4 tablespoons (60 mL) of warm water to the cup.

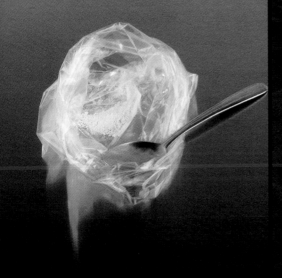

3. Stir for at least half a minute with a plastic spoon. The liquid may be cloudy.

4. Scoop 1 teaspoon (5 mL) of the liquid from Cup 1 and pour it into Cup 2.

continued

5. Add 4 tablespoons (60 mL) of warm water and the iodine to Cup 2. Did the brown iodine turn clear?

6. Add 4 tablespoons (60 mL) of warm water, the hydrogen peroxide, and the liquid laundry starch to Cup 3.

7. Pour all of the liquid from Cup 2 into Cup 3 and start your stopwatch. Now pour the liquid back and forth between Cup 3 and Cup 2 a few times.

8. Set the cup down on a table and watch the liquid. The colorless liquid will turn dark blue in a flash! Check your stopwatch to see how long the reaction took.

9. Now add 2 tablespoons (30 mL) of liquid from Cup 1 into the cup with blue liquid. Stir well. Your dark blue liquid will suddenly turn clear again!

AXIOM EXPLANATION

This experiment may seem like magic—but it's science. It is called an iodine clock reaction. Scientists use clock reactions to study the rates of chemical reactions. They can determine how fast reactants are used up or products appear.

When iodine and starch make contact, they react to form a new dark blue substance. But the vitamin C prevents the iodine from reacting with the starch. The color change will only occur after all the vitamin C is used up. This experiment is a chemical battle between the starch and the vitamin C. The starch wants to make the iodine blue. The vitamin C is trying to stop the blue reaction from happening at all!

SUPER COOL CHEMICAL REACTION ACTIVITIES

WITH MAX AXIOM

_____

_____

_____

_____

_____

_____

_____   _____

_____   _____

_____   _____

_____   _____

_____   _____

SUPER COOL FORCES AND MOTION ACTIVITIES WITH MAX AXIOM

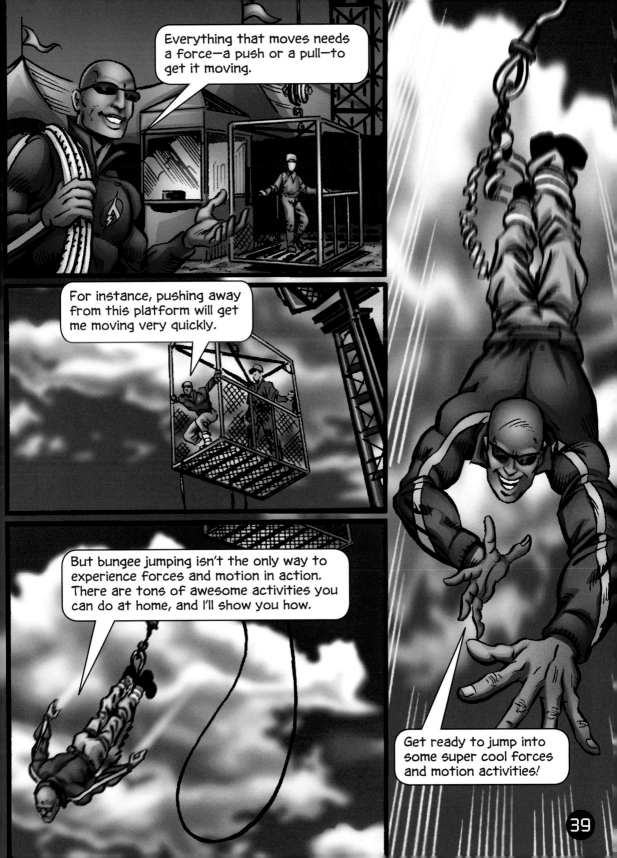

HARD-BOILED DETECTIVE

Almost 400 years ago, scientist Isaac Newton discovered three simple laws of motion. His first law was the law of inertia. It says that an object at rest tends to stay at rest, and an object in motion tends to stay in motion. Use Newton's first law to tell the difference between raw and hard-boiled eggs. You won't even have to crack their shells.

YOU'LL NEED

3 chilled raw eggs

3 chilled hard-boiled eggs

large mixing bowl

PLAN OF ACTION

1. Carefully place all six eggs in the mixing bowl.

2. Use your hands to gently move the eggs around in the bowl. Be careful not to crack the shells as you mix the eggs.

3. Take the eggs out of the bowl and place them on a smooth, flat surface.

4. Spin each egg on its side.

5. Touch each egg lightly to stop it from moving and then let go immediately.

6. Observe how each egg behaves.

⚡ AXIOM EXPLANATION

Did you notice that some eggs wobbled after you stopped them? Those were the raw eggs demonstrating the law of inertia. When you spun a raw egg, the shell began to move. But the liquid inside the shell did not start spinning as soon as the shell did. Likewise, when you stopped a raw egg, the liquid didn't stop moving right away either. Its movement inside the shell made the egg wobble. A hard-boiled egg's solid center, on the other hand, spun and stopped at the same time as its shell.

PENNY DEATH DROP

A resting object's tendency to stay at rest doesn't sound all that exciting. But this super cool coin trick will amaze your friends with the power of inertia.

YOU'LL NEED

cardstock or other stiff paper

ruler

scissors

tape

small jar

water

penny

wooden skewer

PLAN OF ACTION

1. Measure and cut a ¾-inch (2-centimeter) wide by 9½-inch (24-cm) long strip from the piece of cardstock.

2. Form the strip into a hoop and tape the ends together.

3. Fill the jar with water.

4. Place the hoop vertically on top of the jar.

6. Place the skewer through the center of the hoop and very quickly fling the hoop off to the side.

5. Balance the penny on the top of the hoop, over the center of the jar.

7. Watch where the coin goes.

⚡ AXIOM EXPLANATION

If you flicked the hoop fast enough, the coin landed in the water with a splash. But why didn't the coin follow the hoop across the room? Because the coin has inertia. It's at rest while it sits on top of the hoop. When you flick the hoop, the skewer's forward motion is transferred to the hoop, not the coin. The force of gravity pulls the coin down into the jar.

MARSHMALLOW CATAPULT

You may not break down castle walls with this marshmallow catapult, but you will see amazing forces in action. Even better, you'll be able to eat your siege machine when you're done with it!

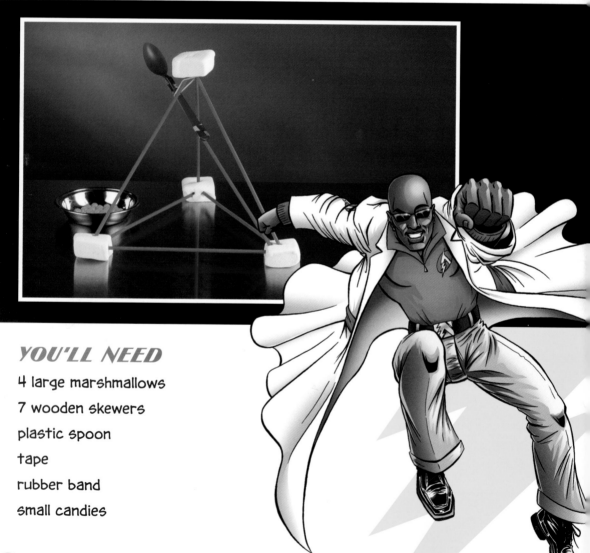

YOU'LL NEED

4 large marshmallows

7 wooden skewers

plastic spoon

tape

rubber band

small candies

PLAN OF ACTION

1. Connect three marshmallows with three skewers to form a triangle. Lay the triangle on a flat surface.

2. Insert one skewer vertically into each marshmallow in the triangle. Angle these three skewers to form a pyramid. Stick the last marshmallow on the point of the pyramid to keep the structure together.

3. Tape the spoon to the end of the remaining skewer.

4. Place the rubber band around the top point of the pyramid.

5. Insert the skewer with the spoon through the rubber band and into one of the marshmallows at the base of the pyramid.

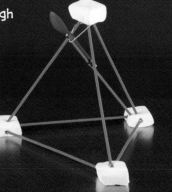

6. Let the catapult sit for at least 24 hours so the marshmallows harden.

7. Place a small candy on the spoon. Gently pull back on the spoon and release to fire the catapult.

AXIOM EXPLANATION

Newton's second law of motion says that when a force acts on an object, the object's movement will change. The more mass an object has, the more force it takes to move it. When you pull the catapult's "arm" back and release it, you apply a force to the candy. That force accelerates the candy across the room. Newton's second law also says that the greater the force on an object, the greater the change in movement. Pull the catapult's arm back more and less to see Newton's law in action.

BOUNCY BALLS

A tennis ball bounces well on its own. But try teaming it with a basketball.
You'll see how momentum turns an ordinary bounce into a super one!

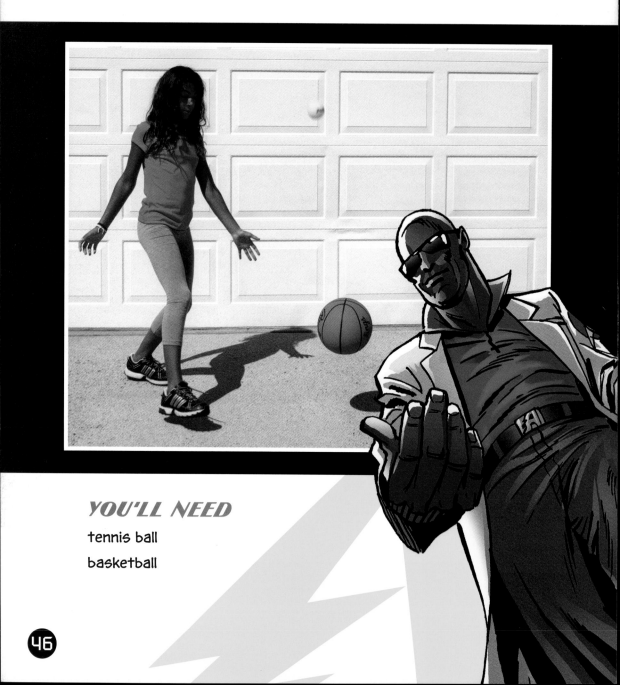

YOU'LL NEED

tennis ball
basketball

PLAN OF ACTION

1. Find an open area of sidewalk or an empty driveway.

2. Drop the tennis ball from shoulder height and see how high it bounces.

3. Drop the basketball from shoulder height and see how high it bounces.

4. Put the tennis ball on top of the basketball, and drop them together from shoulder height again. What happens to the tennis ball?

AXIOM EXPLANATION

Momentum is the measure of a body's motion. It is equal to the body's mass times its velocity. The basketball has more momentum as it falls because it has more mass than the tennis ball. When the basketball hits the ground, some of that momentum passes into the ground. But the remaining momentum passes to the tennis ball. The tennis ball has less mass than the basketball, which means it will gain a greater velocity. This additional momentum sends the tennis ball soaring.

BOTTLE BOAT

Some boats are powered by the wind, others by gasoline. To see Newton's third law of motion in action, you'll power a boat using baking soda and vinegar!

YOU'LL NEED

plastic drink bottle with cap

small scrap of wood

small nail

hammer

1 tablespoon (15 mL) of baking soda

5 marbles

4 ounces (125 mL) of vinegar

large tub of water or bathtub

PLAN OF ACTION

1. Place the bottle's cap on the scrap of wood. Punch a hole in the cap by hammering the nail through it.

2. Place the baking soda inside the bottle.

3. Add marbles to the bottle to weigh it down.

4. Pour in the vinegar and quickly cap the bottle.

5. Tip the bottle so the marbles roll near the cap. Then place the bottle in the tub so the cap is under water.

⚡ AXIOM EXPLANATION

Newton's third law states that for every action, there is an opposite and equal reaction. By actions, Newton meant forces. When vinegar and baking soda mix together, they react and produce carbon dioxide gas. The gas wants to escape through the hole in the cap. The escaping gas pushes against the water and moves the boat forward. The action is the gas rushing out of the hole. The reaction is the boat moving forward.

BALLOON CAR

Rockets use the force of thrust to launch into outer space. You'll use the force of thrust to launch a balloon car across the room.

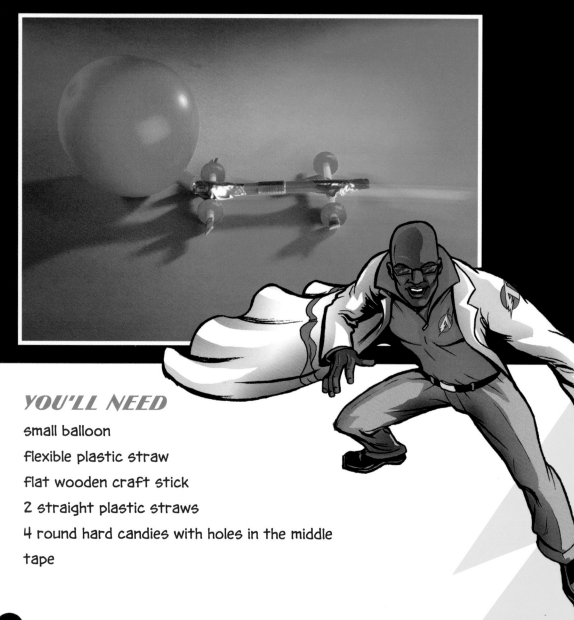

YOU'LL NEED

small balloon

flexible plastic straw

flat wooden craft stick

2 straight plastic straws

4 round hard candies with holes in the middle

tape

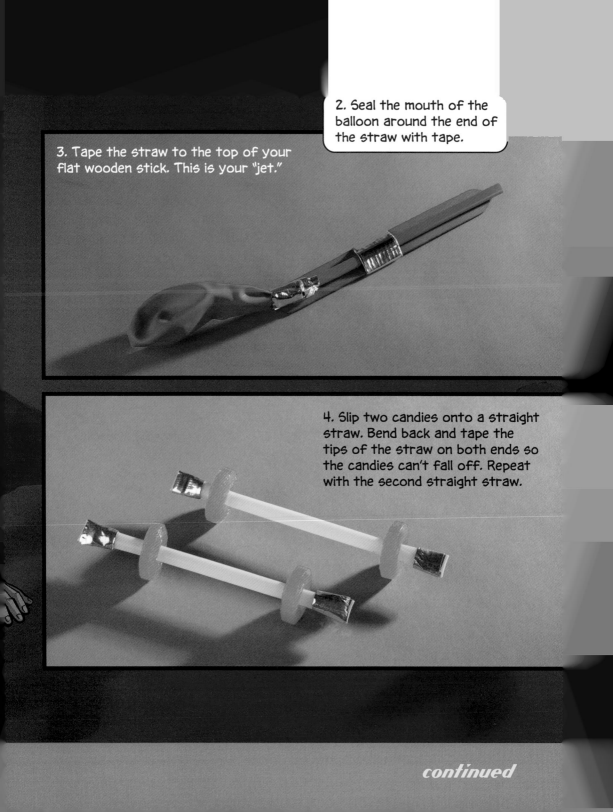

2. Seal the mouth of the balloon around the end of the straw with tape.

3. Tape the straw to the top of your flat wooden stick. This is your "jet."

4. Slip two candies onto a straight straw. Bend back and tape the tips of the straw on both ends so the candies can't fall off. Repeat with the second straight straw.

continued

5. Tape the straws with the candies to the bottom of your flat stick. One should be directly below the balloon. These are your "wheels." Make sure they spin freely.

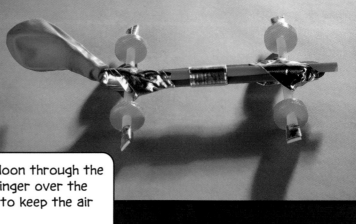

6. Blow up the balloon through the straw. Put your finger over the end of the straw to keep the air from escaping.

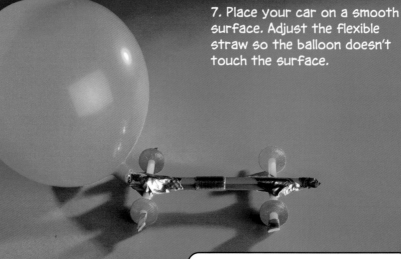

7. Place your car on a smooth surface. Adjust the flexible straw so the balloon doesn't touch the surface.

8. Release your finger from the straw and let the car go.

AXIOM EXPLANATION

Newton's third law of motion is at work once again. The balloon's stored air creates thrust that moves the car forward. When the air in the balloon moves in one direction, it pushes the car in the opposite direction. This is the same way that rockets work. A rocket pushes gas out of its engines. Then the gas pushes back on the rocket and lifts it into space.

FRICTION FUN

Why do people and cars slip and slide on ice? The key is friction—or the lack of it! See how things move differently when friction is reduced.

YOU'LL NEED

cardboard shoebox without lid

scissors

balloon

masking tape

tape measure

notebook

pencil

box of plastic drinking straws

continued

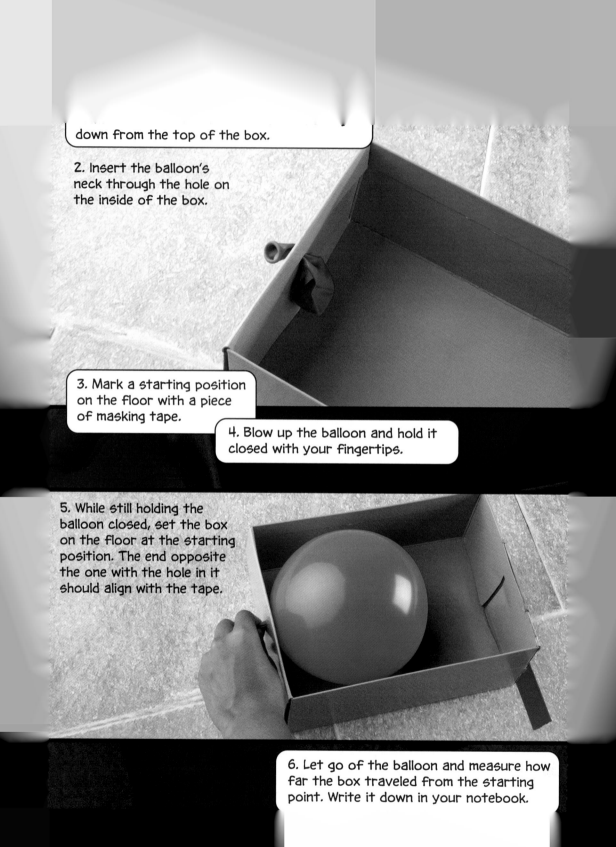

down from the top of the box.

2. Insert the balloon's neck through the hole on the inside of the box.

3. Mark a starting position on the floor with a piece of masking tape.

4. Blow up the balloon and hold it closed with your fingertips.

5. While still holding the balloon closed, set the box on the floor at the starting position. The end opposite the one with the hole in it should align with the tape.

6. Let go of the balloon and measure how far the box traveled from the starting point. Write it down in your notebook.

7. Lay out a "runway" of plastic drinking straws about 3 feet (1 meter) in length starting behind the marked starting position.

8. Inflate the balloon in the box, and holding the balloon closed, set the box atop your runway.

9. Release the balloon. Measure how far the box traveled. Write down your result and compare it to the first.

⚡ AXIOM EXPLANATION

Any time two objects rub against each other, they cause friction. Friction is a force that works against motion. There are different types of friction. On a flat surface, the box is working against sliding friction. But on the straw runway, the box is working against rolling friction. Rolling friction occurs when a round surface rolls over another surface. Your box overcomes rolling friction much easier than sliding friction, so it should have moved farther on the straw runway.

PING-PONG WATER BOTTLE TRICK

Can you feel the pressure? You don't notice it, but the air around you constantly pushes on your body. Check out the surprising power of air pressure with a ping-pong ball and a bottle of water.

YOU'LL NEED

empty glass drink bottle

pitcher of water

plastic tub

ping-pong ball

1. Place the glass bottle in the center of the large plastic tub.

2. Fill the bottle with water until it's overflowing.

3. Place the ping-pong ball on the mouth of the bottle. A little water should come out.

4. Pick up the bottle and carefully turn it upside down over the tub.

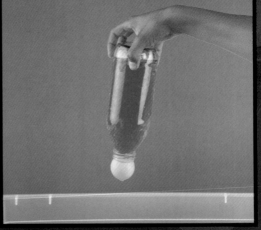

AXIOM EXPLANATION

If the force of gravity pulls on the water and the ping-pong ball, why don't they both fall away from the bottle when you turn it upside down? The answer lies in the shape of the ball. It is a sphere with a lot of surface area. The air pressure all around the sphere keeps the ball in place. Ordinary air pressure is 14.7 pounds per square inch (1 kilogram per square centimeter). It provides enough force to keep the ball sealed to the bottle.

ARTIFICIAL GRAVITY IN A GLASS

Some amusement parks have a ride called the Gravitron. Riders stand against the inner wall of a giant spinning cylinder while the floor drops out. The spinning motion keeps the riders glued against the wall without them slipping down. You can create your own mini artificial-gravity ride using a glass and a marble.

YOU'LL NEED

smooth-sided beverage glass

marble

1. Hold the glass upright by gripping its flat base with one hand.

2. Place the marble in the bottom of the glass.

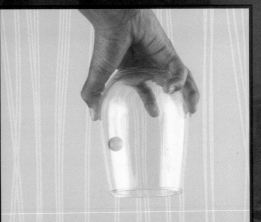

4. While still swirling the glass, tilt it on its side. The marble should continue spinning in a circle.

3. Start swirling the glass so that the marble moves in a circle.

5. Turn the glass upside down as you continue swirling.

⚡ AXIOM EXPLANATION

On a very tiny scale, you've just created artificial gravity! The force that keeps the marble moving in a circle is called centripetal force. Any object in motion tends to stay in motion in a straight line, unless something gets in its way. In this case, the curved shape of the glass makes the marble change direction. At the same time, the friction between the marble and the glass prevents the marble from falling.

GOING MARBLES

Centripetal force keeps you in your seat when you go upside down on a roller coaster. It gives you a push when you're inside a car that's turning quickly. It even keeps satellites from falling out of the sky. But to see actual evidence of this invisible force, all you need is a marble and some gelatin.

YOU'LL NEED

2 clear plastic cups

one-hole paper puncher

duct tape

18 inches (46 cm) of string

pot

measuring cup

1 package of cherry gelatin

1 package of lemon gelatin

marble

flashlight

SAFETY FIRST

Ask an adult to help you make the gelatin because you'll need boiling water.

PLAN OF ACTION

1. Make a hole about 1 inch (2.5 cm) from the top rim of a plastic cup with the paper puncher. Make a second hole directly opposite from the first hole.

2. Stick small pieces of duct tape over the edge of the cup above each hole. The tape should extend to, but not cover, the holes.

3. Thread the string through the holes and tie the ends securely to the edge of the cup.

4. Follow the directions on the package to make the lemon gelatin.

5. Fill the unused plastic cup about halfway full with the lemon gelatin.

continued

6. Place the cup in the refrigerator for about four hours so that the gelatin sets.

7. Remove the cup from the refrigerator and gently press a marble into the gelatin. Allow half of the marble to remain above the gelatin's surface.

8. Follow the directions on the package to make the cherry gelatin. Carefully pour this mixture on top of the lemon gelatin. Leave about 1 inch (2.5 cm) of space at the top of the cup.

9. Place the cup back in the refrigerator for another four hours, until the cherry gelatin is completely set.

10. Remove the cup from the refrigerator and stack it inside the cup with the string attached.

II. Find an open area outside. Hold the string handle and swing the stacked cups quickly for 20 complete revolutions next to your body. Make sure you make a complete circle each time.

…emove the inner cup and … a flashlight through it … …ee how the marble moved.

XIOM EXPLANATION

…he marble should have moved to the bottom of the cup. While the …nts of the cup "want" to move in a straight line, the cup pushes … inward. The tension in the string provides the centripetal force on …p, and the cup provides the centripetal force on the gelatin. Since …elatin isn't completely solid, the marble moves through it until it …es the bottom of the cup. This is the same force that keeps you … in your seat when you're upside down in a loop on a roller coaster.

Lab Notes

SUPER COOL
FORCES AND MOTION
ACTIVITIES
WITH MAX AXIOM

Chapter 3

SUPER COOL MECHANICAL ACTIVITIES

with MAX AXIOM

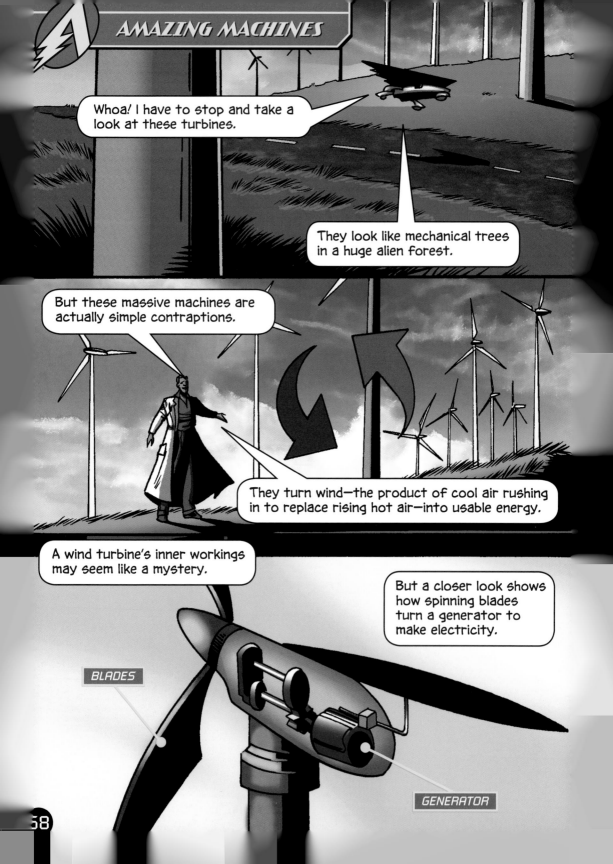

HOVERCRAFT

Wind turbines aren't the only air-powered machines. This peppy little hovercraft glides across your floor on a cushion of moving air.

YOU'LL NEED

hot glue gun

push-top water bottle cap

old CD

large balloon

SAFETY FIRST

Ask an adult for permission to use a hot glue gun before starting this project.

PLAN OF ACTION

1. Place a bead of hot glue along the bottom edge of the bottle cap. Quickly center the cap over the hole in the CD. Hold it in place for about 15 seconds. Push the top of the cap down to close it.

2. Blow up the balloon and pinch the neck closed to seal in the air. Carefully stretch the mouth of the balloon over the top of the bottle cap.

3. Place the hovercraft on a smooth surface and pull up on the bottle cap's push top to open it. Release the neck of the balloon with a gentle push.

4. Watch the hovercraft sail across the surface on a cushion of air.

⚡ AXIOM ALTERNATIVE

Attach the hovercraft horizontally to the back of a small car or set of wheels. See if the machine's backward thrust can push the car forward. Also try cutting fins into a paper plate and using it in place of the CD. Does this change the hover action?

PULLEY SYSTEM

A pulley is a simple machine made of a wheel turned by a rope or a belt. A pulley system helps lift and move objects. Pulleys change the direction and location of pulling or lifting forces. Try out this system to lift and lower an action figure from across the room.

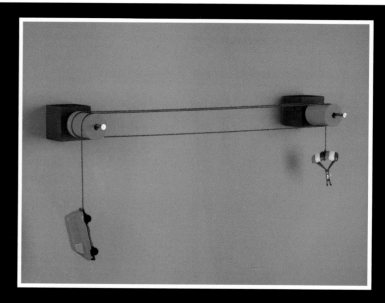

YOU'LL NEED

pencil

4 removable adhesive tabs*

2 2-inch x 2-inch x ¾-inch (5-cm x 5-cm x 2-cm) wood blocks

2 empty thread spools

2 3½-inch- (9-cm-) long nails

hammer

ball of string

scissors

2 small toys

*typically found with adhesive wall hooks

PLAN OF ACTION

1. Ask an adult to help you find an empty wall you can use. Mark two dots at the same height at opposite ends of the wall. At each mark, stick two adhesive tabs with a 1-inch (2.5-cm) gap between them.

2. Place a nail through the center of each spool.

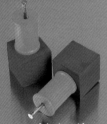

3. Hammer a spool into the center of each of the wooden blocks. Make sure the spools can spin freely.

4. Stick the blocks to adhesive tabs on both ends of the wall.

6. Pull the string under the second spool and guide it back to and around the first spool. Then pull it back to and over the top of the second spool once again.

5. Place the ball of string on the ground under one of the spools. Unwind the string and guide it over the top of this spool. Then carefully pull it to and over the top of the other spool.

7. Let the string hang down to the ground from the second spool. Snip this end of the string off about halfway up the wall.

8. Tie a small toy to each end of the string. Pulling or releasing the figure at either end will do the opposite to the other figure.

AXIOM ALTERNATIVE

This pulley system has more potential than just lifting objects. See if you can use it to send notes back and forth across the room.

DIVING SUBMARINE

Submarines use pumps to fill large tanks, called ballasts, with either air or water. Air-filled tanks make the sub more buoyant and allow it to float to the surface. When the pumps fill the ballasts with water, the sub becomes less buoyant and sinks below the waves. Make your own submarine to see this action at work.

YOU'LL NEED

plastic drink bottle with a push-top cap

utility knife

2 1-inch- (2.5-cm-) diameter washers

4-foot- (120-cm-) long vinyl hose with an outside dimension of 5/8 inch (16 mm) and an inside dimension of 1/2 inch (13 mm)

hot glue gun

tub or pool of water

SAFETY FIRST

Ask an adult for permission to use a utility knife and hot glue gun before starting this project.

1. Use the utility knife to carefully cut two holes on one side of the bottle. The holes should be about the size of a pencil eraser and about 3 inches (7.5 cm) apart.

2. Glue a washer over each of these holes. The washer holes should line up with the bottle's holes.

4. Put the submarine in a tub or pool of water with the hose above the water. Watch the submarine sink as water enters its holes. Make it sink faster by gently sucking on the hose.

5. When the submarine is under water, blow into the hose to make it rise to the water's surface.

3. With the bottle cap opened, slide the hose around its tip. Make sure the hose fits tightly. Use hot glue to seal the hose in place if needed.

AXIOM ALTERNATIVE

Try using a flexible hose and changing the position of the air/water release holes. See if the pump action can move the submarine forward or backward.

PENDULUM PAINTER

A pendulum provides a perfect example of potential energy and kinetic energy in action. When an object on the end of a string swings upward, it gains potential energy. Gravity then pulls the object downward to change the potential energy to kinetic energy. When the pendulum swings upward again, its energy changes back to potential energy. And so the process repeats. Try using pendulum power to paint some super cool designs.

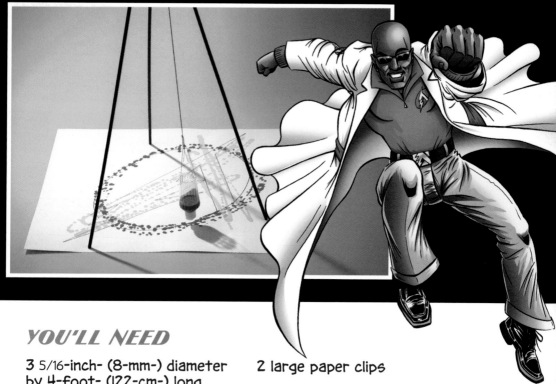

YOU'LL NEED

3 5/16-inch- (8-mm-) diameter by 4-foot- (122-cm-) long wooden dowels

4-foot- (122-cm-) long piece of string

scissors

clean travel size lotion bottle with lid

large sewing needle

2 large paper clips

30-inch- (76-cm-) long piece of string

washable poster paint

water

coffee stir stick

large sheets of paper

1. Arrange the dowels to form a tripod with legs about 2 feet (0.6 m) apart. Let the tops of the dowels cross each other and overlap by about 4 inches (10 cm).

2. Wrap the 4-foot (1.2-m) string tightly around and under the crossing dowels. Continue wrapping until the tripod is tightly bound and its legs stay in position. Tie off the ends of the string.

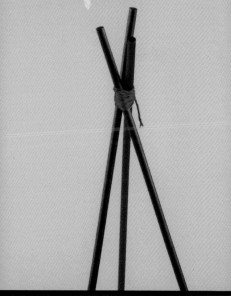

3. Cut off the bottom of the lotion bottle with a scissors.

4. Use the needle to poke two holes on opposite sides of the bottle about ½ inch (1 cm) from the open end.

continued

5. Straighten the middle twist in each of the paper clips. Both paper clips will now have bends on each end.

6. Clip one end of each paper clip through a hole in the lotion bottle.

7. Tie a 1-inch (2.5-cm) loop in one end of the 30-inch (76-cm) piece of string. Tie the other end around the tripod top, leaving the loop hanging down.

8. Clip the paper clip hooks to the loop.

9. With the lid closed, fill the lotion bottle about one-third full with poster paint. Fill another third of the bottle with water. Use the stir stick to mix the paint.

10. Position a large sheet of paper under the painter. Carefully open the cap. Swing and twirl the bottle to watch the pendulum paint a design on the paper.

⚡ AXIOM ALTERNATIVE

Try attaching a second string and bottle with a different color paint. Swing the bottles at the same time to create an even more colorful painting. Try using different lengths of string to see how the design changes.

PUMP DRILL

A pump drill is an ancient tool still used today. It uses momentum created by the spinning motion of a disc placed on a shaft to create a drilling motion. See this amazing pump drill in action for yourself!

YOU'LL NEED

¾-inch (19-mm) x 18-inch (46-cm) wooden dowel

wood saw

2-inch (5-cm) nail

hammer

wire snips

5½-inch x 1½-inch x ¾-inch (14-cm x 4-cm x 2-cm) block of wood

drill

⅞-inch (22-mm) drill bit

⅛-inch (3-mm) drill bit

30-inch- (76-cm-) long piece of string

large plastic coffee can lid

utility knife

electrical tape

piece of scrap wood

SAFETY FIRST

Ask an adult for help when asked to use a drill, saw, or utility knife for this project.

continued

1. Cut a ½-inch (2-cm) deep slit in one end of the dowel with the saw.

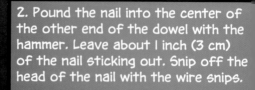

2. Pound the nail into the center of the other end of the dowel with the hammer. Leave about 1 inch (3 cm) of the nail sticking out. Snip off the head of the nail with the wire snips.

3. Drill a hole into the center of the small piece of wood with the 7/8-inch (22-mm) drill bit.

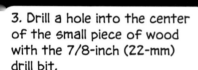

5. Thread one end of the string through one of the small holes. Knot the end. Repeat this step with the other end of the string and the second small hole. Make sure the knots are large enough so they do not slip through the holes.

4. Drill two small holes in the piece of wood with the 1/8-inch (3-mm) drill bit. Each hole should be centered about ½ inch (2 cm) from the ends of the wood.

6. Slide the dowel through the large hole. Insert the string through the slit in the dowel.

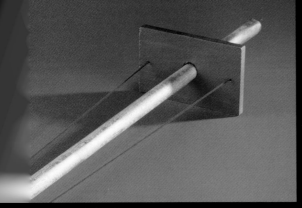

7. Cut a hole through the center of the coffee can lid with the utility knife. Make the hole just large enough so the dowel fits snugly through it.

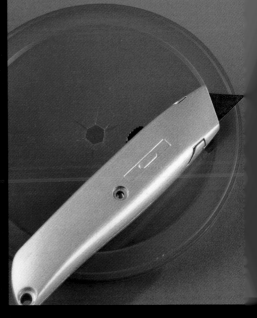

8. Slide the lid up the dowel so that it rests just below the piece of wood hanging on the string. Tape the lid in place.

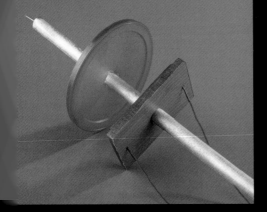

9. Wrap the string around the dowel a few times by turning the piece of wood. Position the pump drill's nail on a piece of scrap wood. Start drilling by pushing the pump drill's wood handle downward. Allow momentum to pull the handle back up before pushing it down again. This momentum will cause the dowel to spin and the nail to drill a hole.

TREBUCHET

A trebuchet was a weapon used in the Middle Ages. This mechanical throwing device uses gravity's pull on a counterweight to fling an object. In a few simple steps, your trebuchet will fling marbles across the room.

YOU'LL NEED

8 large wooden craft sticks

ruler

hot glue gun

2 wooden chopsticks

rubber band

plastic drink bottle cap

drill

1/8-inch (3-mm) drill bit

masking tape

4 l-inch- (2.5-cm-) diameter washers

marble

SAFETY FIRST

Ask an adult for permission to use a hot glue gun and drill before starting this project.

1. Lay three craft sticks out to form a triangle. Overlap their ends so that the ends are flush at two points of the triangle. At the third point, they should overlap each other by 1 inch (3 cm). Glue the sticks in this position.

2. Repeat step 1 with three more sticks.

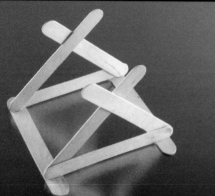

3. Lay the remaining two sticks parallel to each other and about 5 inches (13 cm) apart. Straddle the sticks with the flush sides of the upright triangles, placing them about 4 inches (10 cm) apart. Glue them in place.

4. Form a cross with the chopsticks. Wind the rubber band tightly around the cross to hold the pieces together.

5. Drill a hole in the side of the plastic cap. Slide one end of one chopstick into it. Secure with glue.

6. On the other end of the chopstick with the cap, wrap several layers of masking tape. Slide the washers over the masking tape, making sure they fit very snugly.

7. Set the arms of the cross over the triangle supports. Adjust the rubber band so the washers can swing freely below the crossbar.

8. Pull the cap back and place a marble in it. Release the lid to fling the marble.

⚡ AXIOM ALTERNATIVE

Some trebuchets used a sling instead of a fixed basket. Try replacing the cap with a sling for flinging the marble.

HYDRO-POWERED WINCH

Moving water is a powerful force. Falling water can turn a wheel to generate electricity, run a sawmill, or grind grain. With just a few household supplies, you can build a water wheel winch.

YOU'LL NEED

empty 2-liter bottle

ruler

pencil

utility knife

2 small binder clips

2 thin plastic container lids

scissors

chopstick

12-inch (30-cm) piece of string

tape

small toy

pitcher

water

SAFETY FIRST

Ask an adult for help when asked to use a utility knife for this project.

continued

1. Measure 7 inches (18 cm) up from the bottom of the 2-liter bottle. Mark a line all around the bottle at this height. Carefully cut along this line with the utility knife to remove the top of the bottle.

2. Set the bottle top upside down inside the bottom of the bottle. Clip the binder clips opposite from each other along the edge of the bottle top. Flip the inside handles of the binder clips down.

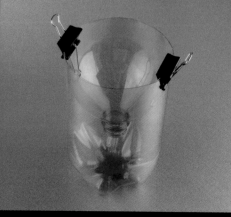

3. Measure and cut two 2¾-inch x 3-inch (70-mm x 76-mm) rectangles from the centers of the plastic lids.

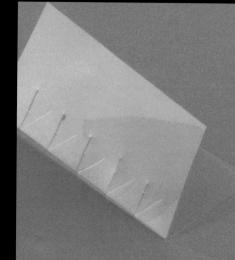

4. Fold one piece of plastic in half along the short dimension.

5. Measure and mark lines every ½ inch (13 mm) along the folded edge.

6. Use a scissors to cut short slits at each mark.

7. Repeat steps 4 through 6 with the other plastic piece.

8. Unfold the rectangles and lay them back-to-back so their slits line up. Weave the chopstick through the slits in both pieces of plastic to hold them together. Spread the four plastic flaps apart to create a water wheel.

9. Slide the chopstick ends through the handles on the binder clips.

10. Tie and tape the string to the longer side of the chopstick. Tie the toy to the end of the string.

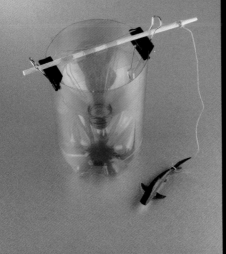

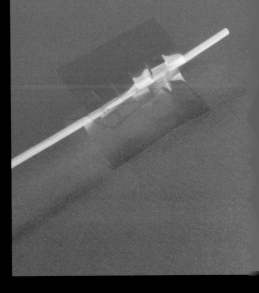

11. Gently pour water from the pitcher onto the center of one of the paddles to turn the winch. As the winch turns it will lift the toy.

AXIOM ALTERNATIVE

Apply moving air to the paddles with a hair dryer. You'll convert the winch from hydropower to wind power. Which has more lifting power, wind or water?

HYDRAULIC ARM

Heavy machinery and many mechanical devices use hydraulic power. Hydraulics use pressurized fluid to lift, push, pull, and dig. Experiment with the power of hydraulics with a simple hydraulic digging arm project.

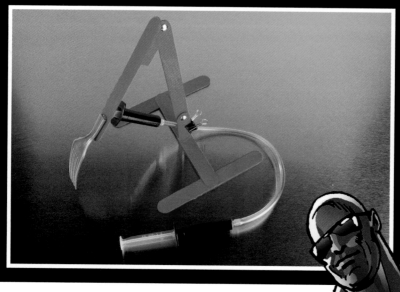

YOU'LL NEED

6 large wooden craft sticks

ruler

hot glue gun

pencil

drill

1/8-inch (3-mm) drill bit

2 brass fasteners

plastic fork

2 syringes

heavy duty shears

12-inch- (30-cm-) long plastic hose with a 1/8-inch (3-mm) inside diameter

small binder clip

SAFETY FIRST

Ask an adult for permission to use a hot glue gun and drill before starting this project.

1. Place two craft sticks parallel to each other. Their outside edges should be about 6 inches (15 cm) apart.

2. Place a drop of hot glue on the center of each stick. Place another stick across the first two to form a letter H. Hold it to the hot glue for about 15 seconds.

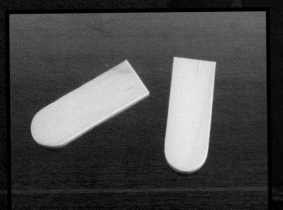

3. Measure and mark a line 2 inches (5 cm) from each end of another stick. Use the shears to cut along each of these lines. Discard the center portion.

4. On one of the 2-inch (5-cm) pieces, measure and mark a dot ¼-inch (6-mm) down from the center of the rounded end. Drill a hole at this dot.

5. Repeat step 4 with the remaining 2-inch (5-cm) piece.

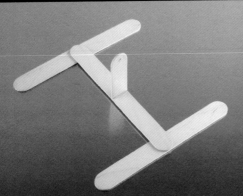

7. Glue one edge of the other 2-inch (5-cm) piece to the center of the flat side of another craft stick. Line up their rounded ends.

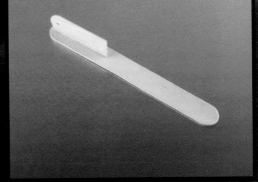

6. Glue the cut end of one of the 2-inch (5-cm) pieces to the center of the H created in step 2. The piece should stand straight up.

continued

8. On the remaining stick, measure and mark a dot a 1/4-inch (6-mm) from the center of each rounded end. Drill holes at each dot.

9. Line up the holes in the long stick with the holes in each of the 2-inch (5-cm) pieces. Connect the pieces with the brass fasteners.

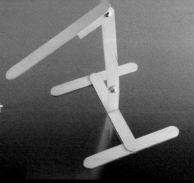

10. Use the shears to cut the handle off the fork and discard it. Glue the fork head, tines down, to the top of the digging arm. The fork should extend off the end of the arm.

11. Insert each of the syringe tips into either end of the hose. Remove one of the syringe's plungers. Close the other syringe's plunger.

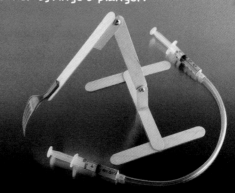

12. With help from a friend, fill the empty plunger with water, pulling the other plunger to fill the hose and syringe. Replace the first plunger. Adjust the syringes so that as one opens, the other closes.

13. Glue the end of one of the plungers to the bottom of the digging arm.

14. Secure the hose to the upright stick with the binder clip. Adjust its location so the arm swings easily up and down when the plunger on the unsecured syringe is pushed or pulled.

AXIOM ALTERNATIVE

For better digging action, try adding a bending joint where the fork attaches to the machine. You can also replace the fork with a spoon for lifting objects, or try adding a paintbrush for painting a design.

ELECTRIC FAN MOTOR

Most motors hide inside the machines they run. But if you could peel back the layers, you'd see an amazingly simple concept at work. Motors use the attracting and repelling properties of magnets to their advantage. An electric current in a loop of wire creates a magnetic field that spins when it is near a magnet. Witness this concept in action by building your own motor-powered fan.

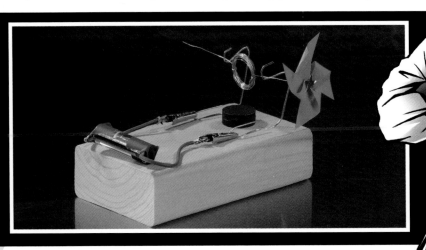

YOU'LL NEED

5 feet (1.5 m) of enamel-coated magnet wire

broom

sandpaper

1½-inch (4-cm) square of paper

scissors

hot glue gun

sewing needle

2 large metal paper clips

needle-nosed pliers

6-inch- (15-cm-) long 2 x 4 board

heavy duty stapler

3 1-inch- (2.5-cm) diameter circular magnets

2 5-inch- (13-cm-) long plastic coated electrical wires

wire-stripping tool

2 small alligator clips

electrical tape

AA battery

SAFETY FIRST

Ask an adult for permission to use a hot glue gun before starting this project.

continued

PLAN OF ACTION

1. Wind the enamel-coated wire around the broom handle at least 15 times. Leave 2 inches (5 cm) loose at each end. Wrap each end twice around the coil on opposite sides to hold the coils together.

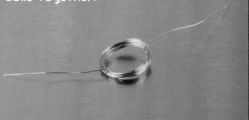

2. Use the sandpaper to sand off all the enamel on one of the 2-inch (5 cm) ends. Sand only one side of the enamel off the other 2-inch (5 cm) end.

3. Cut diagonal slits almost to the center from each corner of the paper.

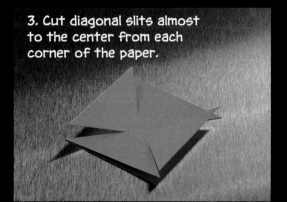

4. Bend the corner of every other paper flap into the center of the paper. Hot glue the corners to the center to make fan blades.

5. Use the needle to punch a hole through the center of the dried hot glue. Stick one end of the coiled wire into the hole on the back side of the fan.

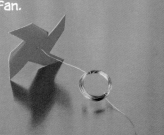

6. Bend one loop of a paper clip at a 90-degree angle. Use the pliers to kink the end of this loop into a small S shape. Repeat with the other paper clip.

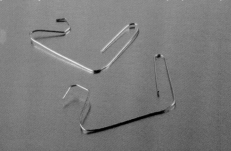

7. Staple the unkinked loops of the paper clips about 2½ inches (6 cm) apart near one end of the 2 x 4.

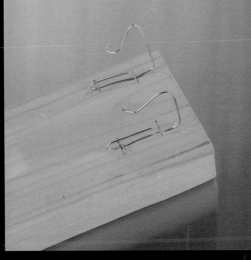

8. Place the wire coil across the paper clip supports. Stack the magnets under the coils.

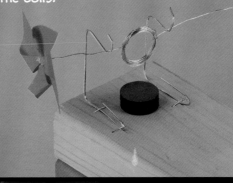

9. Strip about 1 inch (3 cm) of coating from each end of one of the coated wires. Attach an alligator clip to one end. Repeat with the other wire.

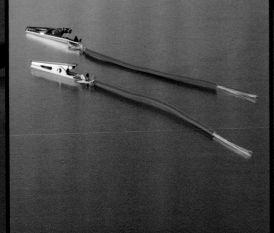

10. Clip each alligator clip to one end of the stapled paper clips. Tape their other ends to opposite sides of the battery.

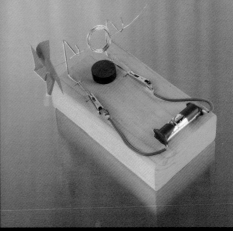

11. Gently flick the wire coil to start it rotating. The fan will begin turning. It can be stopped by unclipping one of the alligator clips.

⚡ AXIOM ALTERNATIVE

Try replacing the battery with a hobby-size solar cell to run the motor using an alternate energy source.

SUPER COOL MECHANICAL ACTIVITIES WITH MAX AXIOM

_____   _____   _____
_____   _____   _____
_____   _____   _____
_____   _____   _____
_____   _____   _____
_____   _____   _____
_____   _____   _____
_____   _____   _____
_____   _____   _____

Chapter 4

SUPER COOL CONSTRUCTION ACTIVITIES WITH MAX AXIOM

It's your turn to build a levee. These large structures are built in a river's floodplain to protect homes and cities. Engineers often combine different materials to improve a levee's strength. Construct your own levee design with a few simple supplies.

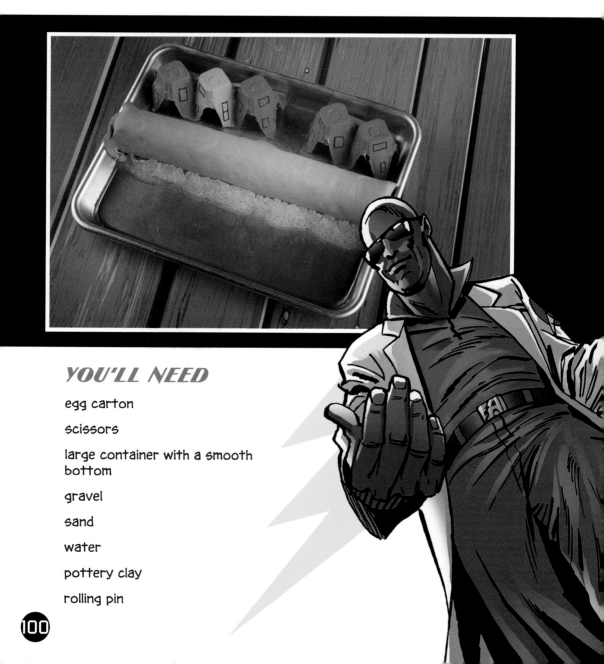

YOU'LL NEED

egg carton

scissors

large container with a smooth bottom

gravel

sand

water

pottery clay

rolling pin

PLAN OF ACTION

1. Using the scissors, cut off four or five egg cups from the egg carton. Place these upside down on one side of the large container. They represent buildings in a floodplain.

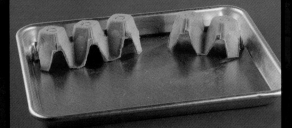

2. Create a wall of gravel 2 to 3 inches (5 to 7 cm) high down the center of the container.

3. Mix a small amount of water with the sand to make it damp. Pack sand around the gravel wall.

4. Roll and pat the clay into a flat sheet long enough and wide enough to cover the levee. Place the sheet over the levee. Smooth it and press its edges to the sides and bottom of the container to form a tight seal.

5. Slowly fill the side of the container opposite the egg cups with water to represent rising floodwaters.

6. Note areas where the wall is weak or leaky. Apply more gravel to make parts of the wall stronger. Add clay to fill in leaks.

AXIOM ALTERNATIVE

Engineers use fabrics called geotextiles to prevent soil from washing away during floods. Try wrapping your levee with pieces of a mesh fruit bag to act like geo-fabric. Does the fruit bag strengthen the levee?

ARCH

Ancient builders often built stone arches without using any cement. How did they do this? The secret is the keystone at the very top of an arch. This wedge-shaped stone holds all the pieces together. Test out the keystone concept with a simple foam arch.

YOU'LL NEED

18-inch (46-cm) square of 2-inch- (5-cm-) thick foam

electric foam cutter

ruler

pencil

SAFETY FIRST

Ask an adult for permission to use an electric foam cutter before starting this project.

PLAN OF ACTION

1. Cut a 5-inch (13-cm) square from the foam.

2. Measure and mark a spot 1½ inches (4 cm) in from one corner of the square. Draw a line from this mark to the opposite corner of the square. Cut along the line to make a truncated triangle.

3. Repeat steps 1 and 2 to make a second identical shape.

4. Draw a trapezoid on the remaining foam. Make it 2 inches (5 cm) along the base, 1½ inches (4 cm) along its top, and 1 inch (2.5 cm) high. Cut out this shape.

5. Repeat step 4 four more times to make additional trapezoids with the same dimensions.

6. Set the truncated triangles upright so they sit about 4½ inches (11 cm) apart. These triangles will be the supports for the arch.

7. Begin stacking the slanted edges of the trapezoids onto the supports to begin forming an arch shape. Stack two on each support, holding them in place as you stack.

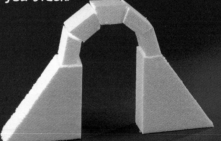

8. Have a friend place the final trapezoid, the "keystone," between the stacks to finish the arch and lock the blocks into place.

⚡ AXIOM ALTERNATIVE

Make additional foam blocks and build a bridge or a span of connected arches. Try doubling or tripling the dimensions of your foam blocks to make larger arches and structures. How tall can you make your arch?

FREEWAY RAMP

A busy city freeway overpass is a web of roads and ramps twisting and weaving around and through each other. Transportation engineers design circular ramps so drivers can safely enter and exit freeways. These ramps must allow cars to make tight turns without crashing or spinning off the road. Test out your engineering skills by building a freeway ramp to keep a marble on a safe course.

YOU'LL NEED

2 30-inch- (76-cm-) long giftwrap tubes

ruler

sharpened pencil

11 unsharpened pencils

2 12-inch- (30-cm-) long paper towel tubes

hot glue gun

12 sturdy paper plates

scissors

packing tape

marble

SAFETY FIRST

Ask an adult for permission to use a hot glue gun before starting this project.

1. Measure and mark 1 inch (2.5 cm), 9 inches (23 cm), 17 inches (43 cm), 23 inches (58 cm), and 29 inches (73 cm) from one end of a giftwrap tube. Use a sharpened pencil to poke a hole at each of these marks. Repeat this step with the other giftwrap tube.

2. Insert unsharpened pencils into the holes made in step 1 to connect the tubes.

3. Mark 1 inch (2.5 cm) from each end of both paper towel tubes. Connect them together as in step 2.

4. Lay the smaller rectangle flat on the floor. Poke holes on the top faces of the tubes, 90 degrees from the first holes. These holes will be perpendicular to the pencils holding the rectangle together. Insert an unsharpened pencil into each of these holes.

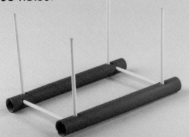

5. Stand the small and large rectangles next to each other. Mark spots where the pencils in the small rectangle touch the large rectangle. Punch holes at these locations and insert the unsharpened pencil ends to make a tower.

6. Adjust the pencils and tubes to make the tower square. Use hot glue to secure the pencils in place.

7. Cut the outside rims from the paper plates. Leave only ½ inch (1 cm) of the flat center part of the plate. Cut away the rest of the plate and discard.

8. Turn one rim upside down and lay it on top of another rim to form a trough. Tape the rims to each other on their undersides. Continue taping rims together to form a long trough coil.

9. Tape one end of the coil to the highest pencil on the tower. Begin winding it around one of the giftwrap uprights. Test each curve by rolling a marble on it to make sure the marble can travel along the curve without flying off. Tape the coil to the upright as you move your way down the structure, constantly testing your roadway.

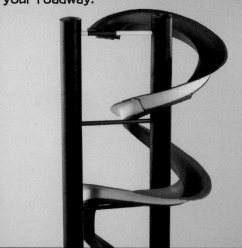

10. When the trough reaches the ground, test the entire structure by rolling a marble from top to bottom. Adjust the trough as needed so the marble follows it all the way down.

AXIOM ALTERNATIVE

Construct another spiraling roadway. Attach it to the other giftwrap upright and connect the roadways. Then race marbles on each of the roadways, trying not to crash them.

SUSPENSION BRIDGE

Suspension bridges use anchored cables to carry the weight of their bridge decks. They are famous for spanning larger gaps than other types of bridges. They easily span distances from 2,000 to 7,000 feet (600 to 2,100 m). Prepare to experience the awesome engineering behind the suspension bridge.

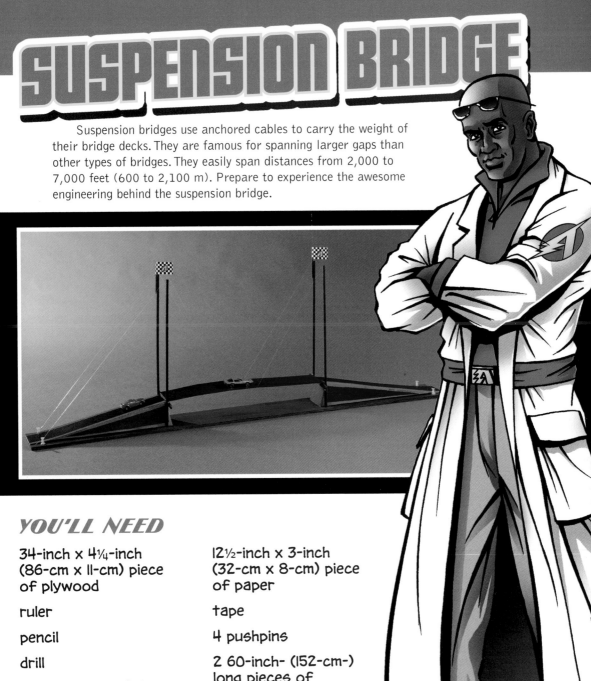

YOU'LL NEED

34-inch x 4¼-inch (86-cm x 11-cm) piece of plywood

ruler

pencil

drill

3/16-inch (5-mm) drill bit

4 wooden skewers

utility knife

hot glue gun

2 wooden craft sticks

12½-inch x 3-inch (32-cm x 8-cm) piece of paper

tape

4 pushpins

2 60-inch- (152-cm-) long pieces of fishing line

empty cardboard cereal box

scissors

continued

PLAN OF ACTION

1. Measure and draw lines ½ inch (1 cm) in from each of the plywood's long edges. Measuring from a short edge of the plywood, make marks at 1 inch (2.5 cm), 11 inches (28 cm), 23 inches (58 cm), and 33 inches (84 cm) on both lines. Ask an adult to drill holes at each of these marks.

2. With an adult's help, use the utility knife to slice a ½-inch (1-cm) slit into the blunt ends of each of the skewers.

3. Insert the pointed end of each skewer into each of the four center-most holes in the plywood. Rotate the skewers so the slits are parallel to the long sides of the plywood. Secure the skewers in place with hot glue.

4. Measure and mark 2 inches (5 cm) up from the bottom of each upright skewer. Place the top edge of a craft stick across each set of skewers at this mark. Glue the craft sticks in place to make two H shapes.

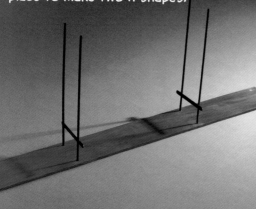

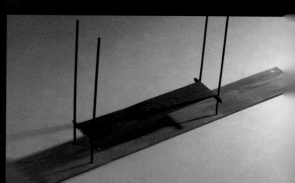

5. Measure and mark a line ¼ inch (0.5 cm) from each short end of the paper strip. Fold the paper at these marks and unfold halfway. Hang the folded edges over the craft sticks. Tape the edges to the craft sticks to make the bridge deck.

6. Firmly push a pin into each of the remaining holes on the piece of plywood.

7. Wrap and tie one end of a piece of fishing line around one of the pushpins. Thread it up through the slit on the nearest upright and under the center of the paper deck.

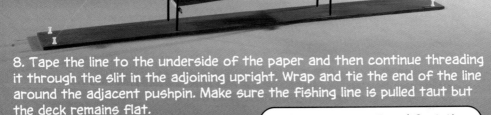

8. Tape the line to the underside of the paper and then continue threading it through the slit in the adjoining upright. Wrap and tie the end of the line around the adjacent pushpin. Make sure the fishing line is pulled taut but the deck remains flat.

9. Repeat steps 7 and 8 at the opposite end of the bridge.

10. Lay the cereal box flat. Measure and mark 2 inches (5 cm) from one corner along the bottom of the box. Measure and mark 10 inches (25.5 cm) from this corner along the side of the box. Draw a straight line between these points. Flip the box and repeat. Cut along these lines to form a wedge.

11. Repeat step 10 with the other bottom corner of the box. Place the wedges at either end of the bridge to form ramped abutments.

12. Place a small vehicle on the bridge to see the suspension cables tighten to hold its weight.

⚡ AXIOM ALTERNATIVE

Experiment with different bridge deck materials. Can you get a cellophane bridge deck to work? Does a cardboard deck make a stronger bridge?

WASTEWATER TREATMENT PLANT

Ever wonder what happens to wastewater when you flush the toilet or drain a sink? Construct a simple two-tank septic system to separate solids and to clean liquids before returning water to the environment.

YOU'LL NEED

2-liter soda bottle

ruler

marker

utility knife

milk jug

14-inch x 8-inch (36-cm x 20-cm) piece of plywood

2 drink straws

hot glue gun

10-inch- (25-cm-) long 2 x 4 board

2 cotton balls

clean sand

clean gravel

small dish

muddy water

SAFETY FIRST

Ask an adult for permission to use a utility knife and hot glue gun before starting this project.

1. Draw an oval that is about 2 inches (5 cm) wide by 5 inches (13 cm) long on the 2-liter bottle. The oval should start at the bottom of one of the bottle's feet. Carefully cut the oval out with the utility knife.

2. Lay the milk jug on its side. Use the utility knife to carefully cut out a large square from its top side.

3. Lay the two straws 2 inches (5 cm) apart on the plywood. One end of each straw should be even with one of the plywood's short sides. Secure the straws in place with hot glue.

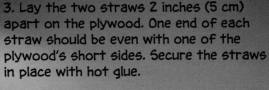

4. Lay the 2-liter bottle between the two straws with the oval hole on top. Make its bottom even with the straw ends.

5. Place one end of the 2 x 4 behind the bottom of the 2-liter bottle. Lay the milk jug on the 2 x 4 with its hole facing up. Allow the jug's spout to overlap the 2-liter bottle's oval hole.

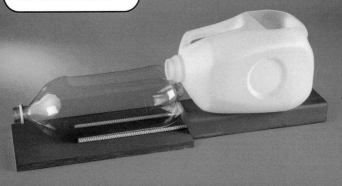

6. Stuff the cotton balls tightly into the neck of the 2-liter bottle.

7. Pack sand into the front end of the bottle, nearest the cotton balls.

8. Fill the rest of the bottle with gravel.

9. Place the dish under the neck of the bottle.

10. Slowly pour muddy water into the hole of the milk jug.

11. Watch as the solids in the water sink to the bottom of the jug. The rest of the water will begin flowing into the soda bottle to be cleaned by the gravel and sand. It will exit the system as clean water. Continue pouring in muddy water.

Each time its level reaches the level of the spout, it will trickle into the gravel. (Although the exiting water looks clean, do not drink it because the system will not remove all the bacteria and chemicals.)

12. Rinse out the solids in the first tank as it begins to fill up.

⚡ **AXIOM ALTERNATIVE**

In a real-life septic system, solids are pumped out as the tank fills up. Design a system to pump out the solids as they collect in the first tank. A hose with a large syringe for a pump might do the job.

HYDRAULIC DRAWBRIDGE

A traffic bridge crossing a shipping channel can pose big problems for ships that are too large to pass under it. Engineers have designed the perfect compromise—the drawbridge. A drawbridge lifts and lowers to allow ships to pass under it. See how it works with this hydraulic-powered drawbridge.

YOU'LL NEED

3 wooden skewers

ruler

pencil

scissors

4 cardboard toilet paper tubes

sharp nail

8 jumbo wooden craft sticks

hot glue gun

2 small eyelet screws

10½-inch x 5½-inch (27-cm x 14-cm) piece of cardboard

2 syringes

12-inch- (30-cm-) long plastic hose with an 1/8-inch (3-mm) inside diameter

SAFETY FIRST

Ask an adult for permission to use a hot glue gun before starting this project.

continued

1. Measure and mark 4½ inches (11 cm) from the blunt end of each of the skewers. Clip off this section with a scissors and discard the rest of the skewer.

2. Measure and mark ½ inch (1 cm) from one end of two cardboard tubes. Poke holes through these marks with the sharp nail. Insert a skewer into the hole in one of the tubes. Stick the other end of the skewer into the hole in the other tube.

3. Measure and make two marks on each of the remaining tubes. Make them ½ inch (1 cm) from one of the ends and ½ inch (1 cm) apart. Punch poles at these marks and connect the tubes with two parallel skewers.

4. Trim one rounded end from six of the craft sticks with a scissors.

5. Lay three sticks from step 4 side-by-side with their square ends even. Repeat with the three remaining sticks. Bring the square ends together.

6. Measure and cut 2-inch (5-cm) sections from the remaining sticks. Lay one 2-inch (5-cm) segment across the joint between the sets of sticks. Glue in place. Lay the remaining 2-inch (5-cm) pieces about 1 inch (2.5 cm) from either end of the sticks. Glue in place to finish the bridge deck.

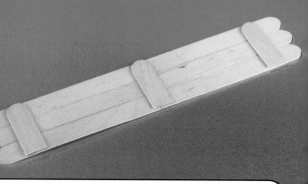

7. Screw the eyelet screws into the center of one of the 2-inch (5-cm) end pieces on the bridge deck. Space the eyelets about 1½ inches (4 cm) apart. Make sure the screws don't pierce the other side of the sticks.

8. Slide out one end of the skewer from the tubes connected in step 2. Thread the eyelets onto the skewer and replace the cardboard tube.

9. Place the whole bridge structure on top of the cardboard piece. Align the tubes in each corner so that their edges are even with the sides of the cardboard. Glue in place.

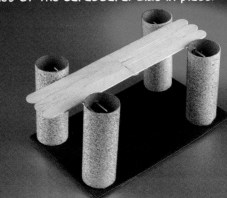

10. Insert each of the syringe tips into either end of the hose. Remove one of the syringe's plungers. Close the plunger on the other syringe. With a friend's help, fill the empty syringe with water. Then pull the other syringe's plunger to fill the hose and syringe with water. Place the plunger back into the empty syringe. Adjust the syringes so that as one opens, the other closes.

11. Insert the back end of one syringe between the skewers from step 3. Allow the syringe's flanges to rest on skewers along the center of their span. Glue the flanges in place.

12. Push and pull the other plunger to raise and lower the bridge.

⚡ AXIOM ALTERNATIVE

Experiment with changing the location of the hydraulics to adjust how far the bridge opens. What happens if you place your hydraulics in the center of the bridge or near the opposite end?

NEWSPAPER PYRAMID

When the Egyptians built the pyramids, they picked a shape they knew could stand the test of time. But why have these structures lasted for thousands of years? Aside from their stone construction, a pyramid's wide base and narrow peak is incredibly stable. Test the strength and stability of a pyramid with a structure made only with newspaper and tape.

YOU'LL NEED

newspaper (30 to 40 sheets)

packing tape

ruler

scissors

stapler

pencil

1. Lay two sheets of newspaper side-by-side with their short sides touching. Tape the short sides together using long strips of packing tape.

2. Tightly roll the sheets diagonally into a tube. Tape the loose corner to keep the tube rolled.

3. Cut about 5 inches (13 cm) from each end of the tube. Wrap a piece of packing tape around each end to strengthen it.

4. Repeat steps 1 through 3 to make three more tubes. Make them the same length as the first tube.

5. Lay three sheets of newspaper side-by-side with their short sides touching. Tape and roll them into a tube in the same manner outlined in steps 1 and 2. Then cut 5 inches (13 cm) off each end of the tube.

6. Repeat step 5 to create three more tubes. Make each of these tubes the same length as the tube in that step.

7. Lay the short tubes in a square shape with their ends overlapping.

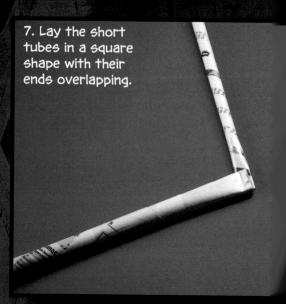

8. Staple the ends together to make the base of the pyramid.

10. Stand up the long tubes and staple their ends together over the center of the square to form the skeleton of the pyramid.

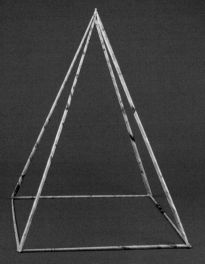

9. Staple one end of each longer tube to one of the base's corners. Make sure the other end of each long tube angles diagonally inward toward the center of the square.

11. Lay several pieces of newspaper side-by-side to form a sheet large enough to cover one side of the pyramid. Tape the papers together.

13. Wrap the newspaper triangle around the tubes and tape it in place.

14. Repeat steps 10 through 12 to cover two additional sides of the pyramid.

12. Lay one side of the pyramid on the top of the newspaper sheets. Trace the outline of the triangle about 1 inch (2.5 cm) larger than the triangle on each side. Cut along these lines.

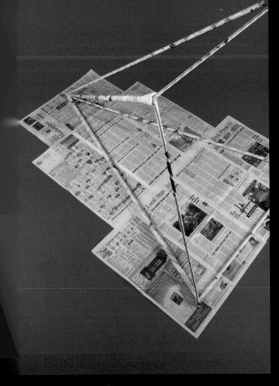

15. Cut a smaller triangle out of a single sheet of newspaper and tape at the top of the remaining side of the pyramid to allow room to crawl into it.

⚡ AXIOM ALTERNATIVE

Compare your pyramid's strength to other newspaper shapes. Try building a cube-shaped fort with the same size base as your pyramid. Which structure is stronger?

LOCK AND DAM

Dams on rivers harness energy to create electricity. They also control water levels to help ships and barges travel safely. But the water levels on opposite sides of a dam often differ by dozens of feet. How do boats safely move from one water level to the other? The answer is a lock system. Float your own miniature boat through a lock and dam system to see how it works.

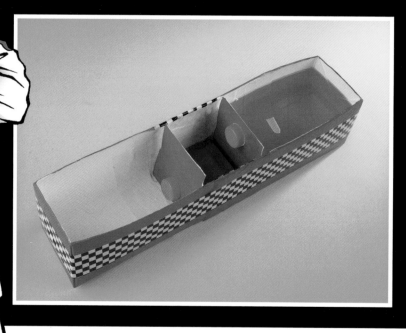

YOU'LL NEED

2 clean 64-fluid-ounce (1.89-liter) juice boxes with screw cap lids

heavy duty shears

ruler

duct tape

foam earplug

PLAN OF ACTION

1. Carefully cut off the glued seam on the top of one of the boxes.

2. Open the box top. Lay it on its side with the spout facing upwards. Carefully cut away the top panel with the spout attached.

3. Repeat steps 1 and 2 with the other box.

4. Lay one box inside the other with their bottoms opposite each other to form a larger rectangular box. Overlap the boxes by about 2 inches (5 cm).

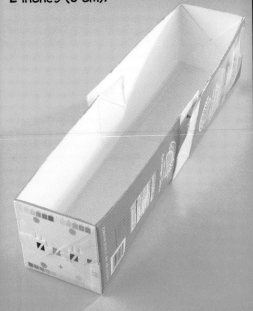

5. Tape the boxes together with strips of duct tape. Tape along the inside overlap and the outside overlap to make the box watertight.

6. Lay one of the pieces of cut away cardboard (with the spout attached) flat. Measure and mark a line parallel to, and 7 inches (18 cm) from, the end nearest the spout. Cut along this line.

continued

7. Measure and mark another line parallel to, and 4 inches (10 cm) from, the end nearest the spout. Bend the spout forward at this line, creasing it at a 90-degree angle.

8. Stand this piece of cardboard inside the box. Place it 7½ inches (19 cm) from one end of the box. The spout should face away from the 7½-inch (19-cm) section you just created. Tape the cardboard in place along all sides to make it waterproof.

9. Lay the other piece of cardboard (with the spout) flat. Measure and mark a line parallel to, and 4 inches (10 cm) from, the end nearest the spout. Cut along this line.

10. Place this cardboard piece upright inside the box 3 inches (8 cm) from the previous piece. The spout should be near the bottom of the box. It should also face the same direction as the other spout. Tape this cardboard piece in place along all sides.

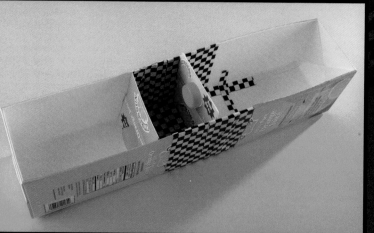

11. Cut the foam earplug in half lengthwise to make a small boat.

12. With the caps on each of the spouts, place the earplug in the first compartment you constructed. Fill this compartment to the top with water. Open the cap to this compartment. Notice how the water level becomes equal in the first two compartments. Gently push the boat through the spout into the second compartment.

13. Open the lower cap. Allow the water level to equalize with the lower pool so the boat can move to the third compartment.

14. To send the boat back upstream, move the boat back to the middle compartment and close the lower cap. Add more water to the first compartment to move the boat back to the higher water level.

15. Adjust the water levels and repeat.

⚡ AXIOM ALTERNATIVE

A river has continuously flowing water that refills each pool as each gate opens. Attach a hose and drain to the system to provide a continuous stream of water to better represent an actual river system.

SUPER COOL CONSTRUCTION ACTIVITIES
WITH MAX AXIOM

_____

_____

_____

_____

_____

_____

_____

_____

_____

_____

Index

Capstone Young Readers is published by Capstone,
1710 Roe Crest Drive, North Mankato, Minnesota 56003
www.capstoneyoungreaders.com

Library of Congress Cataloging-in-Publication Data
Biskup, Agnieszka, author.
  Super cool science and engineering activities: with Max Axiom super scientist / by Agnieszka Biskup
and Tammy Enz.
      pages cm.—(Capstone Young readers)
  Includes bibliographical references and index.
  Summary: "Super Scientist, Max Axiom, presents step-by-step photo-illustrated instructions for
experiments and construction projects related to forces and motion, chemical reactions, mechanical
engineering, and structural engineering"—Provided by publisher.
  Audience: 8–14.
  Audience: Grade 4 to 6.
  ISBN 9781684363049 (paperback)
1. Science—Experiments—Juvenile literature. 2. Engineering—Experiments—Juvenile literature. 3.
Science—Experiments—Comic books, strips, etc. 4. Engineering—Experiments—Comic books, strips,
etc. 5. Graphic novels. I. Enz, Tammy, author. II. Title.
  Q164.B57 2015
  507.8—dc23   2014027880

Editor
Christopher L. Harbo

Art Director
Nathan Gassman

Designer
Tracy McCabe

Production Specialist
Katy LaVigne

Cover Illustration
Marcelo Baez

Project Creation
Sarah Schuette and Marcy Morin

Photographs by Capstone Studio:
Karon Dubke

Printed and bound in the USA. 5046